My Happiness Book

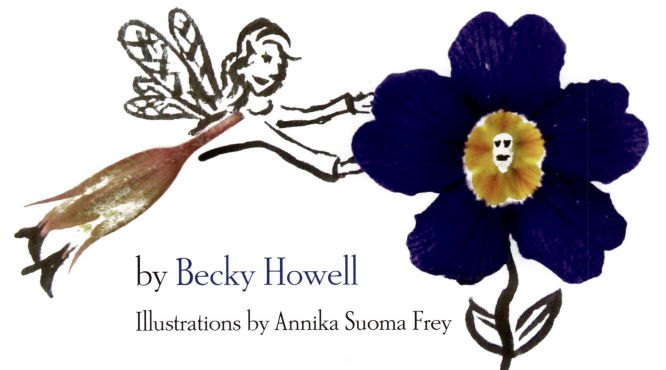

by Becky Howell

Illustrations by Annika Suoma Frey

My Happiness Book
Copyright © 2017 by Becky E. Howell.
All rights reserved.
Printed in the United States of America.
ISBN: 978-0-692-86125-7
No part of this book may be used or reproduced in any manner whatsoever without written permission except in the case of brief quotations embodied in critical articles and reviews. For information go to www.beckyhowell.com.

This book is an exploration in happiness, but is not intended to take the place of professional mental health services or recommendations.

I've done my best to sum up the work of some amazing individuals in just a couple of sentences. Which is not nearly enough. I encourage you to look further into the work of all of the great thinkers mentioned herein.

Dedication

This book is dedicated to my personal happiness teachers:

My maternal grandfather, Don Gunnell, aka 'Bop,' who often referred to happiness as the journey rather than a destination in life.

My maternal grandmother, Barb Gunnell, aka Grandma Nell, who used to say happiness was your song.

My mother, Dona Howell, who believes happiness is a conscious daily choice.

My paternal grandmother, Lucille Whitehead, (Grandma 'Cille to us), who feels you can't be happy without God.

Introduction

My work is focused around healing the Self, holistically. In my coaching practice, I guide my clients into deeper relationships, show them how to release life blocks, and invite peace-happiness-abundance-health into their day-to-day existence.

Children easily experience happiness and gaiety, but happiness seems to elude us adults. It certainly hid from me! It seems that in this chaotic world, being happy is either an obsessive search, or an abandoned and forgotten ideal. I share some of my journey to find happiness with you here, hoping it will help us all shine brighter.

This book will walk you through a few of the philosophical and psychological happiness discoveries down through the ages.

Additionally, you will be asked to take a look at your own happiness journey.

Annika's delightful illustrations will keep us company and open up possibilities to a lighter and brighter state of being.

Shall we travel on together?

What is happiness?

Who came up with the idea?

Where does happiness come from?

Is there one definition of happiness for everyone?

In the fifth century, Buddha encouraged people to leave behind cravings, wants, and desires to enter a peaceful state of mind that left one tranquil

and untroubled like a limpid pool.

Buddha believed happiness was an absence of desires, wants, complications, and expectations.

Do you think happiness occurs in the absence of wants, needs, expectations, goals, and dreams?

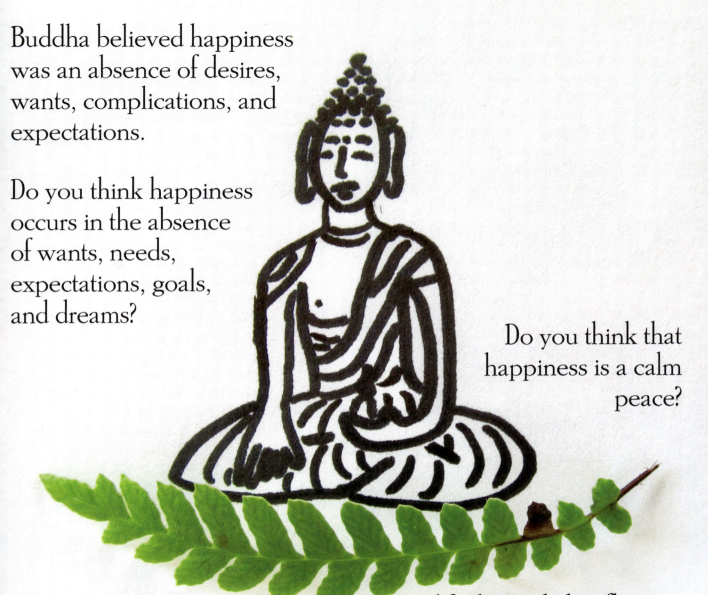

Do you think that happiness is a calm peace?

I have found this type of happiness in my life, but only briefly. In a busy, modern day schedule, this type of peace can sometimes feel elusive.

In the fourth century BCE, Aristotle argued that happiness was the end goal of human existence, and was not attainable before death. Rather, you could look back on a life as being happy if it was lived well.

He believed that having a happy life was the individual responsibility of each person. You could attain this happiness by fulfilling conditions like gaining education, relationships, money, and worthwhile pursuits.

He also believed that life should be spent in rational thinking and virtuous action, in order to become a moral and ethical human, balanced between vices.

I've had several family members pass.
I definitely noticed a different feel to the memorial service when
the person that had passed seemed fulfilled in life,
and so assumed, to be happy.

Do you think you can make your own happiness through
attaining enough virtues and conditions in life?

The word happy first showed up in the English language in the late 14th century. At the time it meant lucky, and was an offshoot of the word hap, like in happenstance, or chance.

About one hundred years later the word happy was flipped into meaning glad, or very glad. This definition suggests happy is a feeling, born from luck, and based on an external event.

Are you able to be happy when things are not going your way?

When you're feeling down on your luck or having a rainy day?

Another way to find happiness is to focus on all the little things that bring you pleasure (also known as hedonic happiness).

What kinds of things bring you pleasure? If you aren't sure, start small: A cup of tea, rainbows, kittens, a new skein of soft yarn, a wonderful brunch with friends.

Maybe it's a good game, a great meal, a sweet kiss, or a brilliant sunset. And then start thinking bigger. A happy relationship. A safe home. Becoming fearless. Gather these gems so that you may always find your way back to your happiness.

It can be challenging to think of things you enjoy when you are down in the dumps.

In that case, look around you. What does your home say?

Is there a common theme to your purchases?
Books?
Or planned holidays?
If someone were to scan your bookcase, what would they know about you?
What feeds your soul?

Eudaemonic happiness is a different approach. This theory says that continually working toward your life purpose is what distinguishes true happiness.

Abraham Maslow was an American psychologist (1908-1970) who subscribed to this purpose-driven happiness theory. He created the Hierarchy of Human Needs triangle, and placed self-actualization as the ultimate human need for happiness. A large part of self-actualization is realizing why we are here, what our purpose is, and realizing our full human potential.

Do you feel clear about your purpose in this *life?*

Try this exercise!

Here is my simple, fill-in-the-blank formula for getting clear on your life purpose:

My purpose is to

_____ (verb: help, show, create, lead)

_____ (noun: specific population, species, location, social movement)

_____ (preposition: by, to, with, for)

_____ (phrase that depicts a unique talent/experience you have).

So you get an idea of what this looks like, I'll share mine:

My purpose is to help humans and horses holistically, by teaching about the four selves (mind, body, spirit, emotions) and how to lead a sustainable, abundant life.

How are you making the world a better place?

Perhaps it helps to divide happiness into categories like Pleasure (life experiences), Work (accomplishing set goals), Belief (being part of a larger enterprise), and Purpose (having a longer view of how you would make the world a better place).

Would having four different categories of happiness make life seem more stable?

Would you still be happy if one, or all, of your categories weren't going well?

We can also look at happiness by dividing it into its most basic feelings. There are as many as 31 common emotions that have been said to contribute to the feeling of happiness!

Emotions like feeling blessed, content, hopeful, loving, and excited.

What emotions do you include with your definition of happy?

What do those emotions feel like on the inside?

Joyful is definitely in my definition of happiness.

The word joy comes from the 12th century. It indicates a deep sense of pleasure or delight and includes both sensual and spiritual elation – without needing an external action to spark the feeling.

Where does happy dance in your body?

We use words to frame our expectations, affirmations, reality, and our journey in this lifetime

It is important to use words meaningfully in order to give weight to our happiness quest.

Choosing our words is the easiest yet most powerful thing we can do to inspire our own metamorphosis into happiness.

What words would you use to describe how you feel when you are at your happiest?

Martin Seligman is a modern-day happiness expert. He was former President of the American Psychological Association, and is partly responsible for shifting the focus of psychology from mental disorders to happiness and quality of life.

Martin suggests that being happy has three graduating levels: a pleasant life, a good life, and a meaningful life.

He says that a pleasant life allows us to enjoy basic life experiences or conditions like good relationships, beautiful sunsets, and music.

A good life is when we delve into who we are and discover our strengths and gifts.

We then use these as tools to make our own existence more comfortable.

A meaningful life is when we use our skills, talents and creativity to help others have better lives as well.

What do you think about this idea of happiness?

Are you able to stay present?

Many people find it difficult, so happiness proves illusive.

If you are dreading or feeling anxious about the future, or regretting and feeling guilty about the past, you cannot completely live in the present which is the only place happiness resides.

Are you able to forgive yourself & others?
Can you view all of your past with gratitude?

Do you view your future with hope & optimism?

William James was born in 1842 in New York. He has been considered the father of American psychology, was an educator, author, physician, philosopher, psychologist, linguist, and explorer.

He reasoned that our beliefs created our reality – and established the link between the mind and body.

James was also famous for realizing that emotions are bidirectional – meaning that we experience them in our bodies as well as our minds.

Happiness is in the Heart ♡

We physically feel dread in the pit of our stomachs, happiness and love in our hearts, and grief in our throats. This is an important concept that bridges our emotions and our body.

If our mind, body, and emotions influence one another, then it stands to reason that sowing conscious, positive thoughts will grow our emotions towards being happy. This yields more smiles.

Only sow what you would harvest

Are you planting seeds of love and laughter so that you may harvest happiness?

Thich Nhat Hanh is a Vietnamese monk, Zen Master, activist, and author born in 1926. He believes that if we can open our eyes to our surroundings, while staying emotionally and mentally present, our happiness will find us!

When we are able to focus intently on the beauty surrounding us - the soughing trees, a sunbeam, your lover's smile - we are moved into happiness by the natural conditions in life.

Thich also suggests that at times our preoccupation with becoming happy can be the very obstacle preventing us from reaching it!

Do you ever feel like you are working hard at being happy? I know I have. That's when its my time to stop and get into gratitude.

If our preconceived notions are rigid, defined, narrow, and unrelenting, we may miss the banquet of glories and opportunities to be happy that are all around us.

Being flexible, aware, conscious, and open allows us to sample many helpings of happiness.

How could your definition of happiness include more helpings?

Deepak Chopra agrees with Thich that becoming attached to impermanent conditions like people, pets, the weather, or a job is unwise.

Everything is illusory and un-possessable except what you have inside.

And yet, it is the very essence of impermanence that makes life itself so perfect and cherished.

It is the process of change through self-improvement and self-discovery that keeps us excited and engaged with life!

Being able to be happy through unsettling change has been a big journey for me. I would reach a happy moment and want it to stretch out for all time. However, I have learned that reliving a frozen moment leads to stagnation, dissatisfaction, and boredom.

Can you view change as a positive, or at least necessary, part of *life?*

Robert Waldinger, a psychiatrist, and Harvard professor, manages the longest running study on adult happiness.

What do you think Professor Waldinger found out about happiness?

The results of the study showed that quality relationships were the key to overall happiness.

Quality relationships means having connections with others and allowing love bonds to grow organically between you.

Relationships are something that I am working to improve. As a loner and introvert, it is easy for me to fall into the trap of believing I don't need any people or help. That relying on others leads to disappointment.

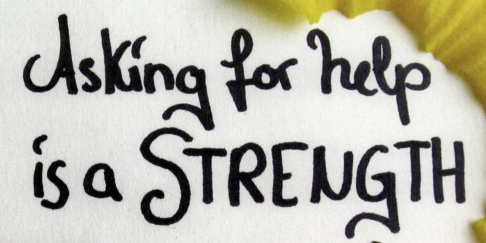

That is like throwing out a whole bushel of apples for the one bad apple at the bottom of the basket.

Are you tossing out lots of good people in fear of finding a few bad apples?

Or are you letting a few negative experiences block you from reaching out?

Dr. Brian King, who brilliantly refuses to admit his age, is an author, psychologist, and comedian in Hollywood. He knows from experience that laughter and happiness are contagious.

When we closely interact with others who are happy

and laughing, we will usually mirror those behaviors ourselves.

We laugh out loud when we are with other people and can feel an organic connection to those around us. When we hide behind mobile devices we become fearful and anxious during honest connections - which leads to fewer chances to experience humor, connection, and laughter.

As Dr. King reminds us, laughing increases our happiness, and our happiness feeds our willingness to laugh.

How can you invite more laughter into your life?

Finally, I wanted to share my own evolving definition of happiness.

For over a decade, I have been working and studying the intersections of mind, body, spirit and emotion in an effort to understand how to be holistically happy and healthy.

I believe that no one definition is sufficient to capture the concept of happiness for all people, in all occasions, for all time.

Each person is a complicated galaxy interacting with numerous other galaxies.

Why would one definition of happiness be simple?

Where is your Balance Point?

I believe that the happiness of each person is a unique balance point between several opposing forces.

What stimulates change and growth in you?

What is important to you?

What brings you joy?

What do you live for?
What would you die for?

Each of us has the freedom, and the responsibility, to discover what forces are essential for us to include in our own definition of happiness.

What forces are you including in your definition of *happiness?*

Check out the accompanying workbook at
www.beckyhowell.com/myhappinessbook

My Happiness Workbook is an easy way to put your happiness into practice.

Thank You

My thank you's are as numerous as the stars in heaven and I am so grateful for the amazing and talented people I am surrounded by.

Annika Frey and I were fated to work together. I saw her doodles one day and was completely hooked and coveted them for my book. Luckily for us all she took the illustration commission and has produced the most delightful little drawings to be included in my book - thank you!

Misti Patrella has been an absolute angel as my book guru, project manager, editor, formatter, and jill of all trades. I relied on her from start to finish. She made this book a magical experience for me - thank you!

A special shout out needs to go to the ladies at Essential Healing, they have been keeping the doors open and our clients happy whilst I have been writing this book and promoting it. They have given me a gift of time to try my hand at new ventures. Thank you Shanna, Jessica, and Katie!

Finally, a very emotional thank you goes to my husband, Adam Berry, my partner through good times and bad and wherever the journey takes us. All my love, forever and always, thank you.

References

Anonymous. "Abraham Maslow." Wikipedia. Wikimedia Foundation, 18 Jan. 2017. Web. 20 Jan. 2017.

Boniwell, Ilona. "The Concept of Eudaimonic Well-being." PositivePsychology.org.uk. Positive Psychology UK, 15 Nov. 2016. Web. 20 Jan. 2017.

Chopra, Deepak. The Seven Spiritual Laws of Success. San-Rafael: Amber-Allen Publishing, 1994. Print.

Hanh, Thich Nhat. How to Love. Parallax Press, 22nd December 2014. Print.

Haybron, Dan, "Happiness", The Stanford Encyclopedia of Philosophy (Fall 2011 Edition), Edward N. Zalta (ed.), URL = https://plato.stanford.edu/archives/fall2011/entries/happiness/

Itkowitz, Colby. "Harvard Researchers Discovered the One Thing Everyone Needs for Happier, Healthier Lives." Washington Post Online, Inspired Life Section, Wednesday, 2nd March, 2016. URL = https://www.washingtonpost.com/news/inspired-life/wp/2016/03/02/harvard-researchers-discovered-the-one-thing-everyone-needs-for-happier-healthier-lives/?utm_term=.aa7495f96d29

Johnson, Pamela Gail. "What is Happiness?" The Secret Society of Happy People Website. 2016. URL = http://sohp.com/what-is-happiness/

Dr. King, Brian. The Laughing Cure, New York: Skyhorse, 2016. Print.

Popova, Maria. "What Is an Emotion? William James's Revolutionary 1884 Theory of How Our Bodies Affect Our Feelings." Brain Pickings. Brain Pickings, 10 Jan. 2016. Web. 20 Jan. 2017.

The Pursuit of Happiness Website, 2016. http://www.pursuit-of-happiness.org/

Skeen, Dan. "Deepak Chopra's Key to Success." Success Television, 2012 Success Media URL = http://successtelevision.com/index.php/Spirituality/deepak-chopra-on-finding-your-lifes-purpose-and-happiness.html

Waldinger, Robert. "What Makes a Good Life? Lessons From The Longest Study on Happiness." Ted Talk. Dec, 2015. URL = http://www.ted.com/talks/robert_waldinger_what_makes_a_good_life_lessons_from_the_longest_study_on_happiness/transcript?language=en

Wall, Alessandra. "10 Things you Should Know About Happy People." Life In Focus. 12 February 2015. URL = http://lifeinfocussd.com/10-things-happy-people/

Becky Howell

Becky Howell is a long-time multipreneur in the Health and Wellness Industry and is constantly searching for holistic ways to help others be happy, healthy, and sustainable. She is an author, coach, and retreat facilitator on a global scale and knows that true power is found inside the self.

You can find Becky on LinkedIn: https://www.linkedin.com/in/beckyhowellcoach

Facebook: https://www.facebook.com/BeckyEHowellHolisticSuccessCoach.

If Becky is conspicuously quiet, she might be continuing her addiction with learning and is on a course somewhere or is recovering as an introvert and hiding in the woods with her horses.

Annika Suoma Frey

Annika lives her life from one soul led adventure to the next while inspiring and supporting others worldwide to do the same.

Her days are filled with love and laughter, making time instead of chasing it and good wholesome food, exploring the wonders of Mother Earth with her husband and her two boys.

You can find Annika at: http://www.lightmaiden.com

CPSIA information can be obtained at www.ICGtesting.com
Printed in the USA
LVIW01n2258160817
545321LV00001B/11